PLANETARY
EXPLORATION

URANUS

KRISTEN RAJCZAK NELSON

Britannica
Educational Publishing

IN ASSOCIATION WITH

ROSEN
EDUCATIONAL SERVICES

Published in 2017 by Britannica Educational Publishing (a trademark of Encyclopædia Britannica, Inc.) in association with The Rosen Publishing Group, Inc.
29 East 21st Street, New York, NY 10010

Distributed exclusively by Rosen Publishing.
To see additional Britannica Educational Publishing titles, go to rosenpublishing.com.

First Edition

Britannica Educational Publishing
J.E. Luebering: Executive Director, Core Editorial
Mary Rose McCudden: Editor, Britannica Student Encyclopedia

Rosen Publishing
Meredith Day: Editor
Nelson Sá: Art Director
Michael Moy: Designer
Cindy Reiman: Photography Manager
Bruce Donnola: Photo Researcher

Library of Congress Cataloging-in-Publication Data

Names: Rajczak Nelson, Kristen, author.
Title: Uranus / Kristen Rajczak Nelson.
Description: First edition. | New York : Britannica Educational Publishing in association with Rosen Educational Services, 2017. | Series: Planetary exploration | Includes bibliographical references and index.
Identifiers: LCCN 2016020469 | ISBN 9781508104216 (library bound) | ISBN 9781508104223 (pbk.) | ISBN 9781508103103 (6-pack)
Subjects: LCSH: Uranus (Planet)—Juvenile literature. | Outer space—Exploration—Juvenile literature.
Classification: LCC QB681 .R35 2017 | DDC 523.47—dc23
LC record available at https://lccn.loc.gov/2016020469

Manufactured in China

Photo credits: Cover Vadim Sadovski/Shutterstock.com (Uranus); cover and interior pages background robert_s/Shutterstock.com; p. 4 Photo Researchers/Science Source/Getty Images; p. 5 Universal Images Group/Getty Images; p. 6 Andrzej Wojcicki/Science Photo Library/Getty Images; p. 7, 18 Encyclopaedia Britannica/Universal Images Group/Getty Images; pp. 8, 20, 23, 25 JPL/NASA;p. 9 Stocktrek Images/Getty Images; p. 10 Mark Garlick/Science Source; p. 11 Space Telescope Science Institute/NASA/Science Source; p. 12 AURA/STScI/NASA/JPL (NASA photo # PIA01280, STScI-PRC96-15); pp. 13, 24, 26 Time Life Pictures/The LIFE Picture Collection/Getty Images; p. 14 Mark Garlick/Science Photo Library/Getty Images; p. 15 Spencer Sutton/Science Source; p. 16 California Association for Research in Astronomy/Science Source; p. 17 Erich Karkoschka, University of Arizona, Tuscon, and NASA; p. 19 AFP/Getty Images; p. 21 NASA/Caltech/JPL; p. 22 U.S. Geological Survey/NASA/JPL; p. 27 NASA/JPL/Caltech (NASA photo #PIA00368); p. 28 Imke De Pater (UC Berkeley) & W. M. Keck Observatory Images; p. 29 Science Source.

CONTENTS

NOT JUST ANOTHER STAR

At its brightest, the planet Uranus is just barely visible to someone on Earth looking up at the night sky. So ancient astronomers could see Uranus—but they could not tell that it was a planet! In contrast, the planets Mercury, Venus, Mars, Jupiter, and Saturn are easily seen shining in Earth's night sky to someone who knows where and when to look. Astronomers could tell that these bright objects were planets by the way they moved.

People on Earth can barely see Uranus (marked in green above) without using a telescope.

After the telescope was invented in the early 1600s, Uranus was seen several times. Those who spotted it, though, thought Uranus was just another star. Then, in 1781, an English astronomer named William Herschel discovered what he thought was a "curious" star or "perhaps a comet." This unusual object soon proved to be a planet—Uranus!

William Herschel built his own telescopes using very large mirrors to observe the night sky.

Like all the planets in the solar system, Uranus orbits the sun. Uranus is the seventh planet from the sun. It is found between Saturn and Neptune. Uranus is called one of the "outer planets" along with Jupiter, Saturn, and Neptune. These are the planets that are found past the main asteroid belt in our solar system.

This illustration shows all the planets in Earth's solar system. However, they would never form a straight line like the diagram shows.

Uranus travels around the sun at an average distance of about 1.8 billion miles (2.9 billion kilometers). It is about 1.7 billion miles (2.7 billion km), or 18.3 **AU**, from Earth. Neptune, the eighth planet from the sun, is about 1 billion miles (1.6 billion km) past Uranus in the solar system.

A
Neptune (30.1 AU)
Uranus (19.2 AU)
asteroid belt (2–4.5 AU)
Jupiter (5.2 AU)
Saturn (9.5 AU)
Venus (0.7 AU)
Earth (1 AU)
Mars (1.5 AU)
Mercury (0.4 AU)
Sun

B
Jupiter (143,000 km)
Venus (12,100 km)
Mars (6,790 km)
Mercury (4,880 km)
Earth (12,760 km)
Neptune (49,500 km)
Uranus (51,100 km)
Saturn (120,600 km)

Jupiter, Saturn, Uranus, and Neptune are called the outer planets. Uranus is the second farthest planet from the sun.

UNIQUE URANUS

One way to know you've spotted Uranus is by its color. Unlike the white-bright stars around it, Uranus looks blue-green! The color comes from the small amount of methane gas in Uranus's atmosphere. The atmosphere is the layer of gases that surrounds the planet. The planet

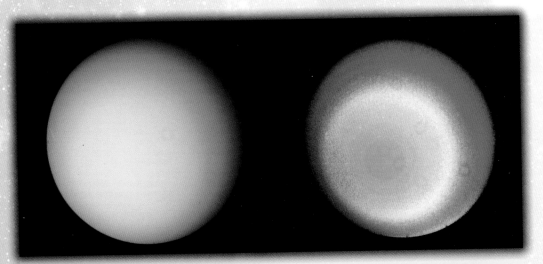

Spacecraft took both images of Uranus. The left shows the planet's colors that are naturally visible to humans. The right was enhanced to show the planet's cloud structure in color.

8

More than sixty Earths would fit inside Uranus. Despite their difference in size, what are some things that Uranus and Earth have in common?

Neptune also looks blue-green because of methane. Uranus is the third largest planet in the solar system, after Jupiter and Saturn. Its diameter is about 32,000 miles (51,000 km). That is about four times the diameter of Earth! Uranus is not very compact. Its density is only about 1.3 times that of water, compared with 1.6 for Neptune and 5.5 for rocky Earth.

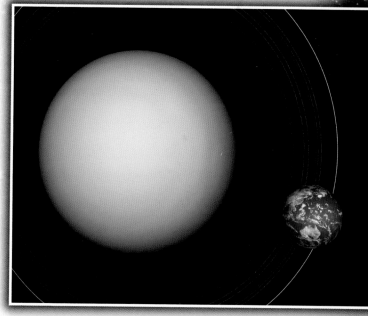

This image compares the sizes of Uranus and Earth by showing them side by side. The two planets never actually come this close to one another as they orbit the sun.

The atmosphere of Uranus is similar to that of the sun and other stars. It is made up mostly of gases, mainly hydrogen and helium. Because of this, it is one of the planets called a "gas giant," along with Jupiter, Saturn, and Neptune. Uranus has no solid surface. But, underneath its huge layers of gases, Uranus has a smaller area of thick, hot liquid.

Uranus is also known as one of the two "ice giants." Neptune is the other ice giant. Both planets contain water, ammonia, and methane, which astronomers call "ices"— even if they are not frozen! High clouds on Uranus are made of frozen methane, and lower clouds

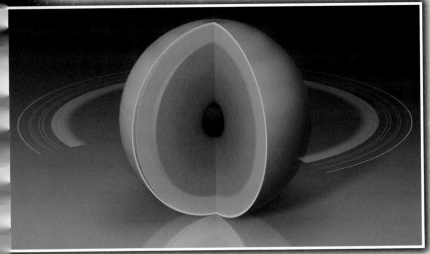

At Uranus's center is a liquid core made up of icy water, methane, and ammonia.

THINK ABOUT IT

Could people live on Uranus? Why or why not?

contain frozen water. In addition, scientists have recorded some very cold temperatures on Uranus. Near the top of its cloud layer, it can be as cold as −366° F (−221° C). However, above the cloud layer in the upper atmosphere, temperatures rise to as high as 890° F (480° C).

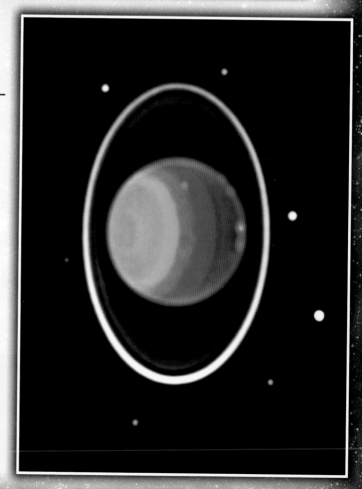

The Hubble Space Telescope took this image. The red spots are storms in Uranus's atmosphere. The storms can be as large as Earth's continents!

RINGS AROUND URANUS

Uranus is surrounded by rings, but they're much fainter than those around Saturn. Uranus's rings were discovered in 1977. Since then astronomers have identified thirteen narrow rings. They are commonly divided into the inner rings and outer rings. As they orbit around Uranus, the rings look very dark, though some are brighter than others.

Uranus's rings are made of many particles, including dust and some

Uranus's rings do not show up well in most pictures. In this image, the rings have been made brighter so that they are easier to see.

ice. Most of these particles are more than 4.6 feet (1.4 meters) across. New dust seems to be constantly introduced into the ring system. The new dust may come from objects, such as meteors, hitting larger particles or moons. In fact, some astronomers think the rings started as a moon—but it broke apart!

A close-up of Uranus's rings shows the large areas of dust and ice particles within the rings.

MOVING AROUND THE SUN

Like all planets, Uranus has two types of motion: orbit and spin. Orbit is the movement of a planet or other celestial body around an object. In our solar system, planets orbit the star we call the sun. The sun's gravity pulls on the planets, keeping them on their orbital path.

Many planets, including Uranus, have an orbit

The illustration shows the planets and other bodies orbiting around the sun. Uranus is on the seventh curved line.

Why do you think it takes Uranus so long to make one trip around the sun?

that is elliptical, or shaped somewhat like an egg or oval. While in orbit, Uranus moves about 15,290 miles (24,607 km) per hour! It takes Uranus about eighty-four Earth years to complete just one trip around the sun. This means that a year on Uranus is about eighty-four times as long as a year on Earth.

The larger the orbital path of a planet, the longer it takes to move around the sun. Only Neptune's orbit is longer than Uranus's.

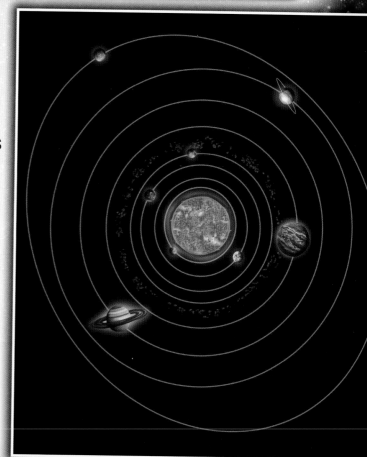

SPINNING SIDEWAYS

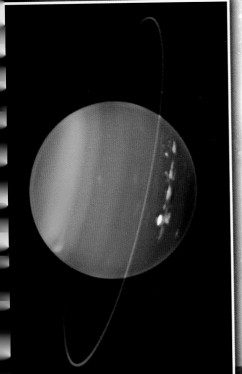

As planets orbit the sun, they also spin. One full spin, or rotation, equals one day on that planet. Each planet spins around an **axis**, which may be tilted any number of degrees in relation to the sun. Uranus's axis has perhaps the most unusual tilt of any planet we know about. It is tilted 97.9 degrees. That means when Uranus spins, it looks like it is nearly on its side!

Scientists think that Uranus may have been knocked into this position early in its history by one or more violent

The tilt of Uranus's axis is unique. No other planet in our solar system has an axis that tilts at such a great angle.

An axis is the imaginary straight line through the center of a planet around which a planet spins.

collisions with other bodies in space. Uranus's spin is unusual in another way, too. It is one of the few planets in the solar system that spins in a clockwise direction around its north pole. Most of the planets spin in the opposite, or counterclockwise, direction.

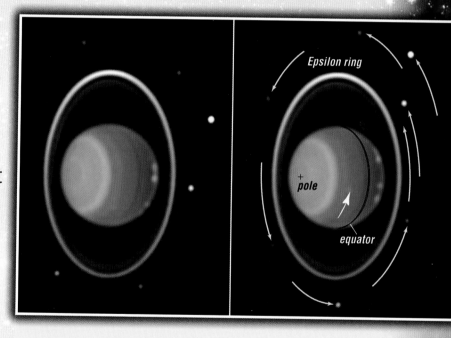

Epsilon ring

+
pole

equator

Uranus spins clockwise around its north pole (counterclockwise around its south pole, shown in these images).

Since Uranus is nearly tipped on its side during its orbit, the sun faces first one of Uranus's poles, then its equator, and then its other pole. This causes the poles of the planet to have many Earth years of sunlight followed by many Earth years of darkness.

Even though its year is longer than a year on Earth, Uranus's day is much shorter than a day on Earth. One full spin of Uranus is only seventeen Earth hours long. It spins very

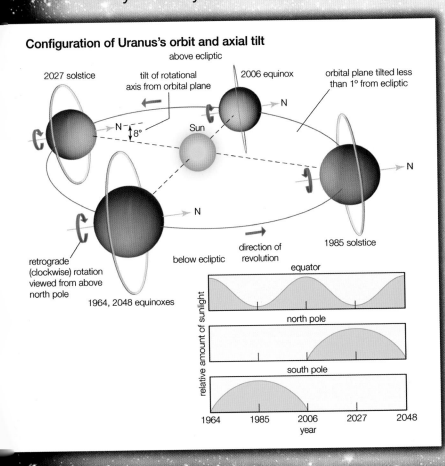

Configuration of Uranus's orbit and axial tilt
above ecliptic

2027 solstice

tilt of rotational axis from orbital plane

2006 equinox

orbital plane tilted less than 1° from ecliptic

N

8°

Sun

N

N

N

retrograde (clockwise) rotation viewed from above north pole

below ecliptic

direction of revolution

1985 solstice

1964, 2048 equinoxes

equator

relative amount of sunlight

north pole

south pole

1964   1985   2006   2027   2048
year

Between 1964 and 2006, Uranus's north pole was in almost complete darkness! Use this illustration to see how that could be possible.

quickly! This quick rotation keeps Uranus from being perfectly round. Its poles are a little flatter, and its equator slightly bulges out as it spins. This happens as Earth spins, too, but not as noticeably as it does on Uranus.

This image was taken by the Hubble Space Telescope in 1994. It shows a clear outline of Uranus's rings and some of its moons.

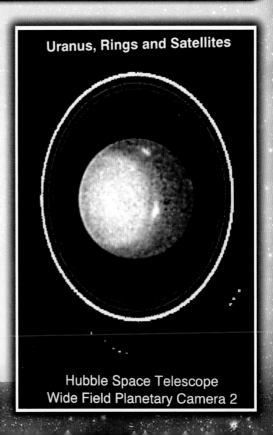

Uranus, Rings and Satellites

Hubble Space Telescope
Wide Field Planetary Camera 2

MOONS

U ranus has twenty-seven moons: five major moons and more than twenty smaller ones. In general, Uranus's rings are located closest to the planet. Some small moons orbit just outside the rings, and the largest moons orbit beyond the smaller ones. Other small moons orbit much farther out beyond the major moons. Uranus's five major moons are named Oberon, Titania, Ariel, Umbriel, and Miranda. The five major moons and

Uranus's five major moons, shown here, were discovered with the use of a telescope from Earth.

COMPARE AND CONTRAST

Earth's moon is made of rock, though some of the rock is solid and some is melted. How is Earth's moon similar to those of Uranus? How is it different?

small inner moons have almost round orbits, while the small outer moons have tilted or very elongated orbits.

Uranus's moons seem to be made up of ice and rock. The four largest are thought to be about 60 percent ice and 40 percent rock. Miranda has a lower density (or is less compact) than the others, so scientists think it might be made of even more ice.

Oberon is the outermost of Uranus's five major moons.

The planet's five major moons range in size from Miranda, which has a diameter of only about 290 miles (470 km), to Titania, which has a diameter of about 981 miles (1,578 km). Some of Uranus's moons have deep valleys and many large pits called craters. Narrow canyons are found on all the major moons. They may have formed by the cracking of the crusts as the moons expanded, or got bigger. Miranda's canyons are the largest, with some being as much as 50 miles (80 km) wide and 9 miles (15 km) deep!

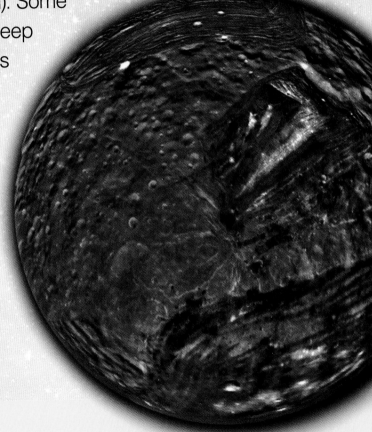

This image shows the many craters found on Miranda, one of Uranus's major moons.

Why do you think Cordelia and Ophelia are called shepherd moons?

Some of Uranus's moons do more than just orbit the planet. Cordelia and Ophelia, two of Uranus's smaller moons, are called shepherd moons. They orbit on either side of one of Uranus's rings. Their gravity helps keep the particles in the ring in place, "shepherding" them as they move around the planet.

Ophelia

Cordelia

This image shows how Uranus's major moons Ophelia and Cordelia follow orbital paths on either side of one of Uranus's rings.

VOYAGER 2 EXPLORES URANUS

Since Uranus's discovery in 1781, astronomers have learned a lot about the planet. Many of the interesting facts about Uranus were not realized until the twentieth century, though. Before 1948, only four of Uranus's moons were known. That year, Miranda was identified. Then, in 1977, Uranus's rings were finally discovered.

In 1986, the National Aeronautics and Space Administration (NASA)

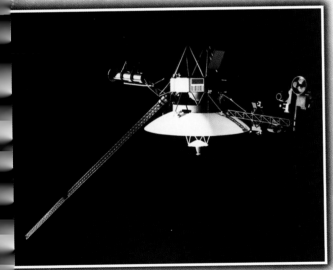

The Voyager 2 probe was launched in 1977. It eventually flew by Uranus in 1986.

sent the unmanned Voyager 2 **probe** toward Uranus and Neptune. Voyager 2 became the first spacecraft to fly by these outer planets. Voyager 2 got about 66,500 miles (107,000 km) from the center of Uranus. It took about eight thousand photographs of Uranus, the first close-ups of the planet and its rings. Voyager 2 also measured the size and mass of Uranus and its moons.

The flight, photographs, and measurements that Voyager 2 took were directed by mission control workers on Earth.

When Voyager 2 first arrived near Uranus, it didn't seem like much was going on. Because of this, some people called Uranus the "boring" planet. But the probe's photographs of Uranus and its moons told scientists a lot about what the surfaces of those bodies were like. Scientists were finally able to study the weather in Uranus's atmosphere, too.

The Voyager 2 mission provided other information about Uranus as well. Until 1986, it was believed that

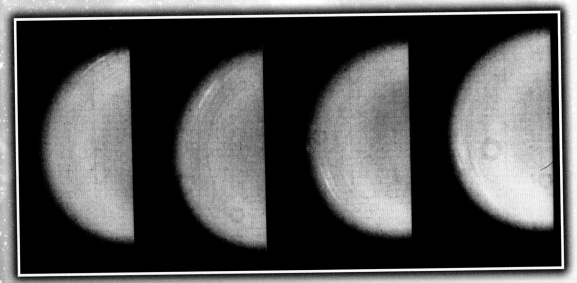

Voyager 2 took these time-lapsed images of Uranus. The bright streaks that change position are clouds. This was the first evidence that scientists had of such features on Uranus.

Voyager 2 was unmanned, meaning there was no person aboard flying it. It takes a probe as many as ten years to reach Uranus. Could NASA ever ask a crew to complete the trip?

Uranus had five moons. Once Voyager 2 flew by the planet, scientists were able to use the probe's data to identify eleven more moons and two more rings. Voyager 2, which had been launched in 1977 to study Jupiter and Saturn, continued on past Uranus to study Neptune as well.

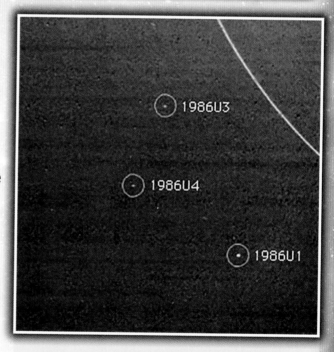

This image shows just three of the moons of Uranus that Voyager 2 helped scientists to identify.

BACK TO THE ICE GIANTS

To date, Voyager 2 remains the only spacecraft to fly by and study Uranus. Since it traveled there, astronomers have been keeping an eye on the blue-green planet using powerful telescopes like the Hubble. More moons have been discovered, and in the early 2000s, storms seemed to be occurring in Uranus's atmosphere. Scientists don't think that Uranus is the "boring" planet anymore!

NASA and other space agencies such as the European Space

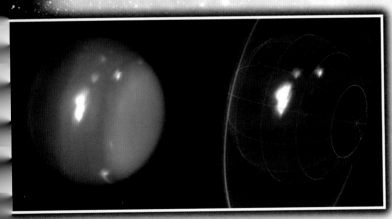

Uranus has become more interesting than ever! The white spots in these infrared images of Uranus are storms.

NASA and other space agencies are trying to build new, more powerful rockets to use for space exploration. What do you think they should explore first?

Agency (ESA) have been pushing to study the outer planets of Uranus and Neptune more. A shared effort between agencies would make funding such a costly mission more affordable. Also, agencies would help one another get the right materials and resources, such as fuel, for the mission. One reason why missions to the ice giants have been proposed is that we still know so little about them. For now, Uranus may remain somewhat of a mystery.

The blue-green Uranus and its many moons have many secrets left for us to uncover!

AGENCY A part of a government that runs projects in a certain area (such as a space agency).

ASTRONOMER A scientist who studies all of the objects outside Earth's atmosphere, including the sun, moon, planets, and stars.

COLLISION The forceful striking together of two objects.

COMET A small chunk of dust and ice that orbits the sun.

DENSITY The mass of something per unit of volume.

DIAMETER The distance through the center of an object from one side to the other.

ELONGATED Lengthened.

FAINT Hard to see.

MAIN ASTEROID BELT The area in space between the orbits of Mars and Jupiter where most asteroids in our solar system are found. An asteroid is a small rocky body that orbits the sun.

MISSION A certain task or job.

PARTICLE A very small part of matter.

SOLAR SYSTEM Everything that orbits, or travels around, the sun. This includes the eight planets and their moons, dwarf planets, and countless asteroids, comets, and other small, icy objects.

TELESCOPE An instrument shaped like a long tube that has lenses for viewing objects at a distance and especially for observing objects in outer space.

TEMPERATURE How hot or cold something is.

TILT A slant.

VISIBLE Able to be seen.

FOR MORE INFORMATION

Books

Deyoe, Aaron. *Moons*. Minneapolis, MN: Super Sandcastle, 2016.

Hutchison, Patricia. *Exploring Beyond Our Solar System*. North Mankato, MN: Child's World, Inc., 2016.

Kruesi, Liz. *Discover Space Exploration.* Minneapolis, MN: Lerner Publications, 2017.

Rhatigan, Joe. *Space: Planets, Moons, Stars, and More!* New York, NY: Random House Children's Books, 2016.

Smibert, Angie. *Space Myths Busted*. North Mankato, MN: 12-Story Library, 2017.

Websites

Because of the changing nature of internet links, Rosen Publishing has developed an online list of websites related to the subject of this book. This site is updated regularly. Please use this link to access this list:

http://www.rosenlinks.com/PE/uranus